Thoughts Whispered from the Heart

Poetry in Short

RAYNE BROWN

DORRANCE
PUBLISHING CO
EST. 1920
PITTSBURGH, PENNSYLVANIA 15238

Dorrance Publishing Co
585 Alpha Drive
Suite 103
Pittsburgh, PA 15238
Visit our website at www.dorrancebookstore.com

ISBN: 978-1-6386-7085-8
eISBN: 978-1-6386-7905-9

Thoughts Whispered from the Heart

Poetry in Short

RAYNE BROWN

TABLE OF CONTENTS

IN MY DEEPEST SPACE

About the Author

I am Rayne Brown. My friends call me Rayne and my siblings' children called me La a. I have blossomed into an intelligent, transparent, and selfless individual. I entered one of my poems in a contest held by the Literary Guild. This poem was printed, but no monetary award was given. I graduated with a Master of Professional Studies but have not obtained a suitable career for my labor. I am certified as a teaching assistant. I work as a teacher aide for a company with elementary school children with special needs.

I learned that expressing feelings is therapeutic. With humility, I share my inner thoughts in spite of circumstances. These writings provided an outlet for healing. Many of my poems relate to personal ordeals. This should have hampered my self-esteem, but I learned that negative situations can be positive.

I was born in Brooklyn, New York. I was raised in the suburbs of Long Island. I am single, never found the right man that I was comfortable with to be my partner. I am the fourth middle sibling of six. We, as a family, had several death tragedies while I was in college. As a whole, life is about elevating yourself, despite negative events. Understand this, I did not share poems to depress my readers. I write in hope to encourage.

II

POEMS

Seed to My Glory

Placed to grow,
Evade the tow.

Foundation at rest,
Never to regress.

Elevating at my best,
Progressing to manifest.

Rebounding the detour,
When life happens, I am unsure.

Re-evaluating my decisions,
I regain my vision.

The seed to my glory
Is the foreseen story.

Half-Baked

Not quite rounded
Because you are bounded,

Your insides are mush,
Always in an empty rush.

Your texture is not complete
To everyone you meet;

You are raw inside,
I cannot deny.

Some are content with your taste
In their distorted haste.

You have the ingredients to shine,
Like vintage wine.

Only you can complete
The procrastination of defeat.

Eyes on You

I love to love what you do;
I love to love my eyes on you.

As the mornings arise, it is no surprise
I love to love what you do.

In noontime,
The sun shines so bright,
I know what's right.

I love to love my eyes on you.

As I look at the dark, peaceful sky,
Reflecting on life, I cannot deny,

I love to love what you do;
I love to love my eyes on you.

Mental Freedom

Dream to me
Or let me be;

Release me from your selfish scheme,
I may dream.

Free me of your shallow words of love.
God above,

He will judge this union of dysfunction.
It takes two for a righteous conjunction.

It takes love and trust,
That is what I desire; a must.

In this sad world of dismay,
It is okay!

To separate,
I will appreciate

Brand new days,
Free from your pretentious ways

Every Day Is Mother's Day!

It is your day;
I am delighted to say

It is your day
in your unique way.

I must express,
No need for you to impress

What you are, every day,
To be blessed.

It is your day,
No need for dismay.

Be one as you are;
There is no other by far.

Every day is your day;
With this note I pray,

This is your day,
All for you.

It is your day,
It is your day,
Happy Mother's Day!

A Message from Rob S.

In the years to come,
Let us learn to have some fun.

Let us love a little more
If someone is on the floor.

Thoughts you cannot ignore;
Do not turn away and shut the door.

Kneel, if you can;
Give that someone a helping hand.

Burned Bridges from Sharon B.

Money can buy lots of people;
Money cannot buy you love or respect.

It is easy to kill a man;
It is hard to make a man.

You can make many enemies within a few seconds
But less than a few real friends in many years.

When a bridge is burned, it is deeper than just words from
      your mouth:
It is the separation of future possibilities;

It is a social tragedy.

The act of burning bridges sears you soul, in ways only your
      subconscious can tell you;
That is, if you listen.

To burn a bridge, any bridge, takes at most a day.
To build a bridge, any bridge, takes at least…years.

Years of development, which include overcoming struggle,
      internal and external.

Solid bridges are earned and not built in a day.
A real relationship, any relationship, includes honesty,
communication, and sharing who you really are.

The result is a bond so sought after and priceless, it is
beyond quantification.

Grateful?

Are you grateful for
Entering my door?

What more do you want?
I placed a mat at the floor.

You have no money;
What do you expect from me, honey?

Are you grateful for
The chores that I have not given?
For you living?

This time,
It is not a crime

To assume you are leaving
In your present, grieving.

My rude words to your demeanor
Are justified.

Are you grateful for
The dishes and grime I left for you?

What do you want me to do?

You have no meaning at this time;
That is the reason for this rhyme.

Maybe next time
You will be grateful for your life;
Not accidentally, not mine.

I, You, Me

You like me,
You hate me,
You love me…

But you want to make me.

You like me,
You hate me,
You love me…

But you want to break me.

You want me,
You flaunt me,
You taunt me;

It is not a crime
At this time

To be what you are
By far.

Control me;
Learn to love me.

Love who I aspire to be. Love,
Who I want to be.

Just love, for me.

In My Blackness!

You view me as bold;
My life has told.

My face is my soul;
My heart will unfold.

I was born with this portrait;
Please do not try to forfeit

Me
The opportunity to express my being,

This life given me.

Pray for my existence,
Ignore my resistance.

You steer from my blackness;
View the mirror and see my blackness.

My face is my blackness;
My soul brings me blackness.
My existence is blackness!

Love is a Weed

Sometimes you make me feel like
A field full of weeds;

Nothing less than animal feed.

When I visualize your arrogant face,
It makes me want to exert to space.

Why bother existing in love
When love to you, is so far from above?

Give love a break
From all your contentious mistakes.

Hope for us, inspire;
Retreat your weed of lust for desire.

In time,

The field of weed
Will embark with lots of sunshine, indeed.

The Non-Committal

Cook for you,
Buy for you,
Care for you…

I am not committed.

Press for you,
Impressed by you,
Laugh with and about you…

I am not committed.

Concerned for you,
Always help you,
Never doubt you…

I am not committed.

Should I commit?
Do I commit?
I do not commit.

I am not committed.

13

A Cool Crowd

In a cool crowd,
Or not afraid to be the fool crowd,
I hear you say, "my dear."

In the cool crowd,
On a whim through town
With no fear,

Carefree in thought and action,
Provocative in appearance, you dare
Not to care.

In the cool crowd,
No one can compare.

What is in the cool crowd?
Not trying to be the fool crowd;

My own individuality is priceless.

In my like crowd,
That is what I want now!
Not trying to be a foot crowd;

In my own crowd,
With my like crowd, not trying to play the fool crowd,
    this time!
I can be myself, that is my cool crowd.

You "be you" crowd,
In your like crowd, that's cool crowd, for you crowd.

To Love a Black Man

You meet,
To greet;

You misread,
Never to lead.

To hang on,
To conquer,

My stature to criticize.
Will you ever realize?

You blame,
No shame,

Much respect for the other;
No regard for your mother.

You scold me;
Just let me be

The rock to your sand,
The concrete to your building.

You fault my being
The cracked paint to your ceiling.

Black man, black man,
Please understand!

I empathize with your pain.
Let me refrain:

I apologize for the scars
Existing from afar.

To love a black man,
This is not a song or dance;

The challenge set forth.
What is it worth?

Does time really heal?
I need to appeal.

Do I love this black man?
I will take a stand,

Love this black wo-man,
Not the troll man;

There is no other
Like some mothers.

Be true to you;
No one else will do.

Look and Taste

Look and taste;
Will not waste

Texture and shape,
Rich tasting as a grape.

Indulgence so sweet,
A gracious meat;

Reluctant to share,
Delicious, I am aware.

Look and taste;
Make no mistake,

I carry the weight,
Existing through my frivolous fate.

Regards to the mindless chase,
Surrender in grace.

Strange Sense

The sweet smell of it;
My what a hit.

No visual look,
Not like reading a book.

The aroma,
A trance to a coma;

It is strange
When your cents are out of range?

The irony of it:
I share this, not at all a hit;

Do not know why
The intensity of being,

In the moment, shy.
Will not deny

I adore it;
A strange bit.

Do not get me wrong;
It can be strong,

Like the toilet to shit,
I welcome it.

Let It Go!

Let it go!
If I may say so,

Time will show,
You need to know,

All the anger and strife,
A mist of life

Let it go!

Life is short;
Let the ship take port.

The words of discouragement,
We need encouragement.

It is a new day;
No time for dismay.

Life has a cost,
Challenging, like weather frost;
Let it go!

And
Let it go!

All Good

So good!
I should say;

If I could,
I may,

I would
Not stray

From you.

To love
Like rain on lawn,

I absorb,
Like lotion to the arm.
What is sacred?

So good,
I should!

It is about that time…
Be mine!

All the time,
In my mind,

Let me be real:
You know the deal.

Mister Uncomfortable

Do not care
To dare;

Will share
My affair.

I am here
With no fear;

I exist,
Like mist.

On a dull day,
Do not pray.

What he strives to be?
I do not see.

Day to day,
I replay,

To be molded
Like clay.

I am Mister Uncomfortable,
Not a superficial double.

20

The Family Not (Knot)

It creates a bind,
Never to unwind;

Secrets from the past,
In memory, forever last.

Aspiring in life is new;
The road to healing is few.

In gathering, we hide,
Mental wounds to inevitably collide.

The superficial camouflage
Of life mirage,

Healing the family knot,
Add a touch of therapy to the pot.

A desire to stir the pot,
Communicating ideas while hot,

Refrain senseless chatter;
Reconcile family matters.

Like our lineage from the past,
Family blessings are vast.

Question Is?

Why do you?
Not like few.

Who are you?
Not like two.

What are you?
Not the moon.

Where are you?
Not in tune.

How are you?
Healing each day.

When are you?
As time play.

The Patch-Up Man

Never to fix,
In others' mix,

Claim by nothing,
Avoids the right thing,

Responsibilities unsure,
Has dissipated from the shore,

The Patch-Up Man
Needs to catch up, man.

Things can mend;
Lots to tend,

For the Patch-Up Man,
Life's no possession.

Pause to Paw

In deep thought
Cause

Two or fours,
Expressly to mourn.

Mouth to muzzle;
It is not a puzzle.

Hurt to heart,
Without a doubt,

Mind set apart,
Reality is the start.

Pause to paw
Cause

Life goes on
Only for the strong.

Two or fours,
Mine or yours.

Bright Eyes

I am bright eyes,
Branded by the family tie,

Innocent at greet,
Hands full of treats.

I am bright eyes
By my family tie;

Every Saturday morn,
preceding the snore,

Our family ties
Regretfully, by

Looking forward to next week.
I continue to seek.

When life happens,
My bright eyes sadden.

Adhere to bright eyes,
Where sincerity lies;

Deep retrospection,
A joyous recollection.

State of Mind

In my state of mind,
I feel far behind,

Ducts in a row
For a career show.

Striving day to day,
My quest to orbit at bay,

Maintaining what I learned
Despite monetary earned.

My state of mind,
Trying to find,

Each day, a new purpose,
Like the hare to tortoise.

My state of mind,
Let me remind,

Realizing the standard;
The life meanders.

In my state of mind,
I seek just cause,

Achieving what I find
Just because.

He Is My Weird

He cares for me,
He does for me,
He keeps for me;

He is my weird.

He annoys me,
He may be strange for me,
He games for me;

He is my weird

All others think
He is strange for me;
You, too, are strange to me.

He will buy the world for me,
But he is my weird.

I love to be,
He is strange to be;

The love he has for me,
He is my weird.

The Dislocated Sole (Soul)

I dislike;
You see,

It is easy
For me.

I care not to shine
In this lonely life of mine.

I speak my mind;
Do not care to rewind.

I care to creep
In my heart, too deep.

I dislike;
You see,

It is easy to me.

I start to care…
But, wait. Do I dare?

I confess to love only two:
My mom and grandma, I do.

I dislike…
Maybe?

It is me against the world;
I may give it a twirl.

Do I let in?
Never to the end.

The Name

What is that name?
It is a trivia game.

Be the same,
Like an animal tame;

Projection of a character,
Like the night of rapture.

A brand engraved on a surface
For the purpose.

What is a name?
Prelude to fame.

Let me explain
My truth, not complain.

Brown to Mandeville
Cast upon a family hill.

Love to Hazy

My life highway,
The spirit that flows
Through me,

The need I have for you
Is not a comedy show;
Its beyond extasy.

You guide me;
We both share
The seas to eternity.

I see us together, one soul,
A gift we both care,
Neither of us have stole.

Throughout our hardship
And separatism,

I hold strength
Given with dignity,

For you,
My world, my destiny.

This may seem crazy,
But this is past love to hazy

Brainwashed

Let me refrain;
Cheers to your brain.

Washed of insight,
Let me take flight.

Your thoughts stained
Succumb to defame;

Your beauty insulted;
Others' mirror resulted.

Every being has a fault,
Pointless to the taste of salt.

Individuality is rare;
No two are a pair.

Celebrate the soul,
That is our human role.

Contentious mold,
The story never told;

Be the brain in wash,
Not the squash.

Free

Free to be me;
Be free, or let it be.

Shall I begin
With a Cheshire grin?

I love this space
Attentive to the face,

Transparent to the eye;
My feelings camouflage to shy,

Aggressive in stature,
Humility to pasture,

Willing to be flexed,
Decisiveness perplexed.

Free to be me,
I do agree,

Doing my part;
Minimize my antagonism, quite smart.

Keeping a level head;
Criticism is dead.

Free to be me,
Maintaining my life, you see.

Cry

I cry;
You, say to me, no emotion,
His immediate notion.

I cry;
With reason, I reply.
You deny.

I cry;
You say, I am weak,
I cannot speak.

You cry,
Expectation to a shoulder;
My emotions colder.

I say,
Sentiment is granted,
Shamefully ranted,

I believe,
Crying to expel feelings,
Momentary healings.

III

ACKNOWLEDGMENTS

Growing up as the fourth sibling of six children was challenging. I never felt comfortable with the person I was. I focused on serving everyone else. I appeared to everyone as a homebody because I never allowed myself to shine. As a graduate student, I related to the "Middle Child Syndrome." Middle Child Syndrome is the belief that middle children were excluded, ignored. Most of the time neglected due to birth order. I started and will be finishing late in life. I come to the understand, it is never too late when accomplishing goals. It's too late when you are deceased.

I would like to thank everyone in my life who inspired me through good or bad encounters. The good and bad experiences allow me to direct negative to positive. Life is the obstacle. I am growing and learning each day to inspire through past and projected experiences.